mini cakes

& other bite-size treats

mini cakes
& other bite-size treats

Hannah Miles

photography by William Lingwood

RYLAND
PETERS
& SMALL

LONDON NEW YORK

Dedication
For my mum and dad, with love.

Senior Designers Megan Smith and
Sonya Nathoo
Senior Commissioning Editor Julia Charles
Head of Production Patricia Harrington
Art Director Leslie Harrington
Publishing Director Alison Starling

Prop Stylist Liz Belton
Food Stylist Lucy McKelvie
Indexer Hilary Bird

First published in 2011 by Ryland Peters
& Small
20–21 Jockey's Fields, London WC1R 4BW
www.rylandpeters.com

10 9 8 7 6 5 4 3 2 1

Text © Hannah Miles 2011
Design and photographs © Ryland Peters
& Small 2011

ISBN: 978-1-84975-146-9

Printed and bound in China

A CIP record for this book is available from the
British Library.

US library of Congress Cataloging-in-
Publication Data has been applied for.

Author's acknowledgements
A big thank you to all at RPS – in particular
to Julia Charles my wonderful editor; Megan
Smith and Sonya Nathoo for the lovely design;
and Lauren Wright for the fabulous PR support.
Thanks also go to Lucy McKelvie for the elegant
food styling and William Lingwood for the
wonderful photographs. Huge hugs to
Giancarlo Caldesi who continues to be my
great foodie mentor and much love to all my
wonderful food taster friends and family – Jane,
Geoff, Charles, Maren, Gareth, Amy, Mike, Liz,
Jess, Josh, Rosie, Miles, Tina, Lucy, David, Kathie
and the Kimbolton School Chamber Choir.

contents

small is beautiful

The latest trend sweeping New York bakeries and Parisian pâtisseries is mini baking – adorably tiny versions of cakes and desserts, designed to tantalize the tastebuds in just one mouthful. Perfect for afternoon tea parties, elegant dinners and as a sweet canapé at a drinks party, mini cakes also make welcome and thoughtful gifts. All your favourites, from iced éclairs and French fancies, to pecan pies and blueberry bundts, are included here but all on a miniature scale. As well as being delightful to look at and delicious to eat, these tiny morsels can be enjoyed without guilt as they have all the taste of a large slice of cake or serving of dessert but only a fraction of the calories!

Each chapter of this book contains different types of bite-size bakes – from pretty-as-a-picture sponge cakes to light-as-air pastries. Also included are recipes for small desserts – just right for serving as a pre-dessert or why not create a fashionable trio of recipes to give your guests the ultimate in indulgent treats?

All the recipes in this book can be baked using mini cupcake, muffin, bundt and tartlet pans, which are widely available from good cookware stores. A piping bag with a selection of tips is useful for achieving the prettiest finish, but otherwise an oven and standard kitchen equipment is all you need. So why not don your apron, grab your whisk and whip up a batch of delightfully tiny treats today!

cakes

These pretty little pastel sponge cakes topped with sugared petals are just perfect. Tiny morsels of sweet cake, delicately scented with rose and violet, they will delight any afternoon tea party guest.

French fancies

115 g/1 stick butter, softened

115 g/½ cup plus 1 tablespoon caster/granulated sugar

2 eggs

115 g/¾ cup plus 1 tablespoon self-raising/rising flour

1 tablespoon plain yogurt

1 teaspoon vanilla extract

BUTTERCREAM

300 g/2 cups icing/confectioners' sugar

30 g/2 tablespoons butter, softened

1–2 tablespoons milk

4 tablespoons violet liqueur

TO DECORATE

500 g/3¾ cups powdered fondant icing sugar

2 tablespoons rose syrup

pink and blue food colouring

candied rose and violet petals

a cake tin/pan (20 cm/8 in square), greased and lined

a piping bag fitted with a small round nozzle/tip

20 mini paper cases

makes 20

Preheat the oven to 180°C (350°F) Gas 4.

To make the sponge cake, whisk together the butter and sugar until light and creamy. Add the eggs and whisk again. Sift in the flour and fold in, along with the yogurt and vanilla extract. Spoon the mixture into the prepared pan and bake in the preheated oven for 20–25 minutes, until the cake is golden brown and springs back to the touch. Let cool.

To make the buttercream, whisk together the icing/confectioners' sugar, butter, milk and 1 tablespoon of the violet liqueur until light and creamy. Trim away the sides of the cake then cut the cake in half horizontally. Place one half on a tray that will fit in the fridge. Drizzle the remaining violet liqueur over the sponge cake and spread over a thin layer of buttercream. Top with the other half and cover the top and sides with a thin layer of buttercream. Using a sharp knife score the top of the cake into 20 squares (do not cut through to the cake). Spoon the remaining buttercream into the piping bag and pipe a small blob of buttercream in the middle of each square. Chill in the fridge for 2 hours, until the buttercream is firm, then cut the cake into the marked squares.

Put the fondant icing sugar in a saucepan with 3–4 tablespoons water, rose syrup and a few drops of pink food colouring. (Add the water gradually as you may not need it all.) Put the cakes on a wire rack with foil underneath to catch the drips. Spoon the warm icing over half of the cakes, ensuring each cake is covered completely. When you have iced half the cakes, add a few drops of blue food colouring to the remaining icing to make a lilac colour and cover the remaining cakes. Decorate each cake with a rose or violet petal and let set before putting in paper cases. The cakes will keep in an airtight container for 3 days.

What could be nicer than having a whole layer cake all to yourself?
Decorated with tiny handmade fondant strawberries, these little
treats are pretty-as-a-picture and perfect for any summer tea party.

strawberry & cream layer cakes

115 g/½ cup plus 1 tablespoon
    caster/granulated sugar
115 g/1 stick butter, softened
2 eggs
85 g/⅔ cup self-raising/
    rising flour
30 g/⅓ ground almonds
1 teaspoon vanilla extract
300 ml/1¼ cups double/heavy
    cream, whipped
200 g/1½ cups strawberries,
    thinly sliced
3 generous tablespoons
    strawberry preserve

TO DECORATE
30 g/1 oz. ready-to-roll icing
red and green food colouring
    pastes
200 g/1⅔ cups powdered
    fondant icing sugar
1 tablespoon rosewater

10 mini cake tins/pans
    (6 cm/2½ in diameter),
    greased

makes 10

Preheat the oven to 180°C (350°F) Gas 4.

In a mixing bowl, whisk together the sugar and butter until light and creamy. Whisk in the eggs then sift in the flour. Fold in along with the almonds and vanilla extract. Spoon the mixture into the pans and bake in the preheated oven for 15–20 minutes, until the cakes spring back to the touch. Let cool in the pans then slide a knife around the edge of each one to release the cakes.

To make the fondant strawberries, colour three quarters of the ready-to-roll icing red with a small amount of red food colouring paste. Colour the remainder with the green food colouring paste. Make at least 40 tiny strawberry shapes with the red icing and use a sterilized pin to prick holes in them to look like the seeds. Top each with a tiny blob of green icing to represent the stalks. Set aside to dry.

To prepare the icing, mix together the fondant icing sugar, rosewater and about 1 tablespoon cold water until you have a smooth, thick icing. Cut each cake into 3 layers and cover the top layer of each cake with icing. Allow the icing to set for about 5 minutes and then gently press 4 fondant strawberries on to the top of each one to decorate.

Once the icing has set completely, assemble the cakes. Spoon a little whipped cream and preserve between each layer, topping with strawberry slices. Finish each one with an iced and decorated top.

Serve immediately or store in the fridge until needed.

These dainty bite-size scones are filled with peach preserve, fresh nectarines and raspberries and cream for a decadent teatime treat.

peach melba scones

100 g/¾ cup self-raising/ rising flour
1 teaspoon baking powder
30 g/⅓ cup ground almond
30 g/2 tablespoons butter, chilled and cubed
2 teaspoons almond extract
30 g/2 generous tablespoons caster/granulated sugar, plus extra for sprinkling
2–3 tablespoons milk

TO SERVE
3–4 tablespoons clotted cream or whipped double/heavy cream
1 nectarine, thinly sliced
16 raspberries
3 tablespoons peach preserve
icing/confectioners' sugar, for dusting

a scone cutter (5 cm/2 in diameter)
a large baking sheet, greased and lined

makes 16

Preheat the oven to 180°C (350°F) Gas 4.

Sift the flour and baking powder into a mixing bowl and add the ground almonds. Rub the butter into the flour mixture with your fingertips, until it resembles fine breadcrumbs. Add 1 teaspoon of the almond extract, the sugar and 2 tablespoons milk and mix to form a soft dough. Add a little more milk if the mixture is too dry.

On a flour dusted surface, use a rolling pin to roll out the scone dough to a thickness of 2 cm/¾ in and stamp out 16 rounds using the cutter. Put the scones on the baking sheet a small distance apart. Using a pastry brush, glaze the tops of the scones with the remaining milk mixed with the remaining 1 teaspoon almond extract. Sprinkle with sugar.

Bake in the preheated oven for 10–15 minutes, until golden brown and the scones sound hollow when you tap them. Let the scones cool on a wire rack then cut each one in half and fill with a little clotted cream, nectarine slices, a few raspberries and a little peach preserve. Replace the tops of the scones and dust with icing/confectioners' sugar to serve. Serve immediately or store in the fridge until needed.

All the comfortingly indulgent flavours of rocky road ice cream — chocolate, nuts and marshmallows — are encapsulated in these treats.

rocky road slices

60 g/⅓ cup caster/granulated sugar
60 g/½ stick butter, softened
1 egg
60 g/½ cup self-raising/ rising flour
1 tablespoon buttermilk
30 g/1 oz. dark chocolate, grated
150 ml/⅔ cup double/heavy cream, whipped

CHOCOLATE GLAZE
30 g/2 tablespoons butter
60 ml/¼ cup light corn syrup
70 g/2½ oz. dark chocolate, broken into pieces

TO DECORATE
mini marshmallows
glacé Cherries, halved
white chocolate chips
chopped walnuts

a 20-cup/hole silicone mini loaf tray/pan, greased
a piping bag fitted with a large star nozzle/tip

makes 10

Preheat the oven to 180°C (350°F) Gas 4.

Whisk together the sugar and butter until light and creamy. Whisk in the egg. Sift in the flour and fold in, along with the buttermilk and grated chocolate. Spoon the mixture into the loaf pan and bake in the preheated oven for 10–12 minutes, until the cakes spring back to the touch. Let cool in the pan.

To prepare the chocolate glaze, heat the butter, syrup and chocolate in a saucepan until the chocolate has melted. To assemble, spoon the whipped cream into the piping bag. Turn out the cooled cakes from the pan and pipe small stars of cream onto half of the cakes. Top with the remaining cakes and cover with the chocolate glaze.

Decorate the cakes with the mini marshmallows, cherries, white chocolate chips and walnuts. Pile as high as you can for the best effect. Serve immediately or store in the fridge until needed.

60 g/⅓ cup caster/
   granulated sugar
60 g/½ stick butter
1 egg
60 g/½ cup self-raising/
   rising flour
1 teaspoon baking powder
60 g/½ cup blueberries,
   quartered
finely grated zest of 2 lemons

BLUEBERRY DRIZZLE
250 g/2½ cups blueberries
juice of 2 lemons
150 g/¾ cup caster/
   granulated sugar

24 mini bundt ring tins/pans
(7 cm/2¾ in diameter), greased

makes 24

Traditional German Bundt cakes are popular the world over. Bundt pans are ring pans usually decorated with patterned edges and it is important to grease the pans well so that the cakes release. Topped with a blueberry drizzle and fresh berries, these tiny bundts are almost too cute to eat!

mini blueberry bundts

Preheat the oven to 180°C (350°F) Gas 4.

Put the sugar and butter in a mixing bowl and beat together until light and creamy then whisk in the egg. Sift in the flour and baking powder and gently fold in, along with the quartered blueberries and lemon zest. Spoon the mixture into the prepared pans and bake in the preheated oven for 12–15 minutes, until the cakes spring back to your touch. Remove from the pans and let cool on a wire rack.

To make the blueberry drizzle, cut 50 g/½ cup of the blueberries in half and put them in a pan with the lemon juice. Heat gently until the blueberries are very soft and have released their juices. Strain through a sieve/strainer, pressing down on the fruit to release all the juices. Return the strained juice to the pan, add the sugar and stir over the heat until the sugar is dissolved. Drizzle over the cakes and fill the central holes of the cakes with the remaining fresh blueberries to serve.

The undrizzled cakes will keep in an airtight container for 2 days.

These dainty cakes decorated with little pairs of 'wings' are pure temptation. Flavoured with tangerine and filled with a tangy passion fruit mousse, this recipe takes a classic kids party cake to a new level.

butterfly cakes

60 g/½ stick butter, softened
60 g/⅓ cup caster/granulated sugar
1 egg
60 g/½ cup self-raising/rising flour
1 teaspoon baking powder
finely grated zest of 1 tangerine or 1 small orange
orange sprinkles, to decorate

PASSION FRUIT MOUSSE
5–6 ripe passion fruit
115 g/½ cup plus 1 tablespoon caster/superfine sugar
60 g/½ stick butter
2 eggs
200 ml/¾ cup double/heavy cream, whipped

a 12-hole/cup mini muffin tin/pan lined with paper cases
a piping bag fitted with a small star nozzle/tip

makes 12

First make a passion fruit mousse. Cut the passion fruit in half and scoop the flesh into a fine mesh sieve/strainer. Press with the back of a spoon to release all the juices then discard the seeds. Measure 80 ml/⅓ cup of juice, pour into a microwave-proof bowl and add the sugar and butter. Microwave on full power for 3 minutes, stirring half way through. Beat the eggs and whisking all the time, beat slowly into the hot passion fruit mixture. Return to the microwave for about 1 minute, stirring half way through, until the mixture is thick and glossy. Alternatively (if you do not have a microwave) put the passion fruit, butter and sugar in a heatproof bowl and set over a saucepan of gently simmering water. Whisk until the sugar has dissolved. Add the eggs a little at a time, whisking continuously, until the mixture is thick and glossy. Pass it through a sieve/strainer to remove any lumps. Set aside to cool completely.

To make the cakes, preheat the oven to 180°C (350°F) Gas 4. Cream together the butter and sugar until light and creamy. Beat in the egg, sift in the flour and baking powder and fold in, along with the tangerine zest. Put 2 spoonfuls of mixture in each paper case. Bake in the preheated oven for 10–15 minutes, until the cakes are golden brown. Turn out onto a wire rack to cool.

When you are ready to serve, fold the cooled passion fruit mixture through the whipped cream and spoon into the piping bag. Gently slice the top from each cake and cut in half to create 'wings'. Use an apple corer to cut a hollow in each cake. Pipe a swirl of the passion fruit mousse into the hole in each cake, top with a pair of 'wings' and decorate with sprinkles. Serve immediately or store in the fridge until needed.

- 60 g/¼ cup (packed) soft dark brown sugar
- 60 g/½ stick butter, softened
- 1 large egg
- 60 g/½ cup self-raising/rising flour
- 1 teaspoon ground cinnamon
- 1 teaspoon ground mixed spice/apple pie spice
- 1 teaspoon vanilla extract
- finely grated zest of ½ an orange
- 1 medium carrot, peeled and cut into chunks
- 30 g/¼ cup unsalted pistachio kernels
- 30 g/¼ cup walnut pieces
- 1 generous tablespoon long shredded coconut

CREAM CHEESE FROSTING
- 50 g/¼ cup cream cheese
- 25 g/2 tablespoons butter, softened
- 85 g/½ cup icing/confectioners' sugar
- finely grated zest of ½ an orange
- 20 edible carrot cake toppers, to decorate (optional)

a 24-hole/cup mini muffin tin/pan, greased
a piping bag fitted with a large star nozzle/tip

makes 20

Who doesn't love a slice of moist carrot cake with a fluffy, cream cheese frosting. These mini mouthfuls are packed with pistachios, walnuts and coconut and make a delightfully wholesome anytime treat.

mini carrot muffins

Preheat the oven to 180°C (350°F) Gas 4.

In a mixing bowl, whisk together the brown sugar and butter until light and creamy. Whisk in the egg and then sift in the flour, cinnamon and mixed spice/apple pie spice. Fold in along with the orange zest and vanilla extract. Put the carrot chunks, pistachios, walnuts and coconut in the food processor and chop very finely. If you do not have a food processor, grate the carrot and chop the nuts finely using a sharp knife. Fold the carrot mixture into the cake mixture until everything is incorporated.

Spoon the mixture into the prepared muffin pan and bake in the preheated oven for 12–15 minutes, until the muffins spring back to the touch. Turn out onto a wire rack to cool.

To make the cream cheese frosting, whisk together the cream cheese, butter, icing/confectioners' sugar and orange zest. Spoon into the piping bag and pipe a swirl of frosting on top of each muffin. Top each muffin with a carrot cake topper (if using).

The cakes will keep in an airtight container in the fridge for 3 days.

7-g/¼-oz. sachet fast-action
    dried yeast
100 ml/⅓ cup warm water
85 g/⅓ cup caster/granulated
    sugar
500 g/4 cups self-raising/
    rising flour
a pinch of salt
200 ml/¾ cup sour cream
1 egg
60 g/½ stick butter, chilled
2 teaspoons ground
    cinnamon
1 teaspoon vanilla extract
about 1 litre/4 cups vegetable
    oil, for deep-frying

VANILLA BUTTER GLAZE
250 g/1¾ cups icing/
    confectioners' sugar
60 g/½ stick butter
1 teaspoon vanilla extract
sprinkles, to decorate

CINNAMON SUGAR
about 200 g/1 cup caster/
    superfine sugar
1 tablespoon ground
    cinnamon

*a small, round cutter
(2 cm/1 in diameter)
2 baking sheets, lined with
baking parchment*

makes 60

These doughnuts take a bit of effort but are definitely well worth it. They are finished two ways – with vanilla butter glaze or dusted in cinnamon sugar – both equally yummy.

ring doughnuts

To make the doughnuts, put the yeast, warm water and 3 teaspoons of the sugar in a bowl. Leave in a warm place for 10 minutes, until a foam forms on top. Sift the flour and salt into a mixing bowl and rub in the butter with your fingers. Add the egg, sour cream, cinnamon, vanilla extract and yeast mixture to the bowl and mix with your hands to form a dough. Knead until the dough is pliable and soft, using a little extra flour if too sticky. Leave the mixture in a warm place in a bowl covered with a damp kitchen cloth for 1 hour, until the dough has doubled in size.

Knock the dough back and form sixty 5-cm/2-in balls of dough. Press each ball down gently and stamp a hole out of the middle using the cutter. Put the rings a distance apart on the baking sheets, cover again with damp kitchen cloths and leave for 30 minutes, until doubled in size.

Heat the oil in a large saucepan. Drop a small piece of bread into the oil – if it floats and turns golden brown the oil is ready. Cook the doughnuts in batches for about 2–3 minutes on each side, until golden brown. Remove with a slotted spoon and drain on paper towels.

To make the vanilla butter glaze, heat the icing/confectioners' sugar, butter, vanilla extract and 60 ml/¼ cup water in a saucepan, stirring all the time, until the butter has melted. Put foil under a wire rack to catch any drips and dip half of the doughnuts in the glaze in the pan and then transfer to the rack using a slotted spoon. When the first coat of glaze has set, reheat the glaze and return the doughnuts to the pan for a second coat and then leave to set on the rack, adding sprinkles (if using).

For the cinnamon sugar doughnuts, mix the sugar and cinnamon and toss the warm doughnuts in the mixture. Serve warm or cold. These doughnuts are best eaten on the day they are made.

115 g/1 stick butter, softened
115 g/½ cup plus 1 tablespoon
   caster/granulated sugar
2 eggs
115 g/¾ cup plus 1 tablespoon
   self-raising/rising flour
2 tablespoons buttermilk
100 g/¾ cup finely chopped
   dried apricots
50 g/1½ oz. white chocolate,
   finely chopped
3–4 tablespoons apricot
   preserve
28 sugar toadstools and
   edible glitter, to decorate

CHOCOLATE GANACHE
200 g/6½ oz. dark chocolate
80 ml/⅓ cup double/heavy
   cream
1 tablespoon light corn syrup
30 g/2 tablespoons butter

BUTTERCREAM
50 g/scant ½ cup icing/
confectioners' sugar
1 tablespoon soft butter
2 teaspoons milk
green food colouring

*a loose-based cake tin/pan
(18 cm/7 in square), greased
and lined
a round cutter (4 cm/1½ in
diameter)
a piping bag fitted with a
leaf nozzle/tip*

makes 14

These white chocolate and apricot cakes, smothered in a rich chocolate ganache and topped with adorable sugar toadstools would grace any fairytale-themed birthday party buffet.

chocolate pixie cakes

Preheat the oven to 180°C (350°F) Gas 4.

   In a mixing bowl, whisk together the butter and sugar until light and creamy. Whisk in the eggs. Sift in the flour and fold in, along with the buttermilk, apricots and white chocolate. Spoon the mixture into the prepared pan and bake in the preheated oven for 20–25 minutes, until the cake springs back to the touch and a knife comes out clean. Turn out onto a wire rack to cool and then stamp out 14 small rounds of cake with the cutter. Heat the apricot preserve in a saucepan set over gentle heat and then brush over the top and sides of each cake with a pastry brush to seal in the crumbs.

   To make the chocolate ganache, put the chocolate, cream, syrup and butter in a heatproof bowl set over a saucepan of simmering water (making sure that the base of the bowl does not touch the water). Stir until the chocolate is melted and you have a thick sauce. Put foil under the wire rack to catch the drips and spoon the chocolate ganache over each cake, ensuring that the sides are completely covered.

   To make the buttercream, whisk together the icing/confectioners' sugar, butter, milk and a few drop of green food colouring until creamy. Spoon into the piping bag and pipe leaves on the top of each cake. Finish each cake with two toadstools and sprinkle with edible glitter.

   The cakes will keep in an airtight container for 2 days.

pastries

Eclairs, traditionally topped with chocolate and filled with cream, are one of those 'naughty but nice' indulgences. These bite-size éclairs, topped with chocolate, coffee or peppermint-flavoured fondant icings and filled with a sweet Chantilly cream, are as dainty as can be.

baby éclairs

Preheat the oven to 200°C (400°F) Gas 6.

Heat the butter in a saucepan with 150 ml/⅔ cup cold water until the butter is melted. Bring to the boil, then quickly add the sifted flour all in one go and remove from the heat. Beat hard with a wooden spoon or whisk until the dough forms a ball and no longer sticks to the sides of the pan. Leave to cool for about 5 minutes. Whisk the eggs and then beat into the dough a small amount at a time using a balloon whisk. The mixture will form a sticky paste which holds its shape when you lift the whisk up. Spoon into the piping bag and pipe 30 small lines about 5 cm/2 in long onto the baking sheet, a small distance apart. With clean hands wet your finger and smooth down any peaks from the piping so that the pastry is smooth. Bake in the preheated oven for 10 minutes, then with a sharp knife cut a small slit into each éclair and return to the oven for a further 3–5 minutes, until crisp. Cool on a wire rack and then cut each in half.

To make the chantilly cream, whip the cream and vanilla seeds until the cream reaches stiff peaks. Sift in the icing/confectioners' sugar and fold through gently. Spoon the cream into the remaining piping bag and pipe into the éclairs.

To make the icings, mix the fondant icing sugar with 2 tablespoons water and divide into three bowls, colouring each with a very small amount of food colourings and/or flavourings of your choice. Spread the icing onto the éclairs using a round-bladed knife and let set before serving. Serve immediately or store in the fridge until needed.

CHOUX PASTRY DOUGH
50 g/3½ tablespoons butter, chilled and cubed
65 g/½ cup plain/all-purpose flour, sifted twice
2 eggs, beaten

CHANTILLY CREAM
300 ml/1¼ cups double/heavy cream
seeds from 1 vanilla bean
about 1–2 tablespoons icing/confectioners' sugar

To DECORATE
250 g/1¾ cups powdered fondant icing sugar
3 food flavourings and/or colourings of your choice

2 baking sheets, greased and lined
2 piping bags fitted with round nozzles/tips

makes 30

Religieuse is the French word for nun and these cute choux buns are said to resemble nuns in their habits. Be as adventurous as you like with the decoration – the traditional finish is cream piped in vertical lines and a silver dragee, but rosettes of cream look equally pretty.

rose petal religieuses

1 quantity Choux Pastry
   Dough (see page 27)

ROSE CREAM
2 tablespoons rose syrup
500 ml/2 cups double/heavy
   cream

FONDANT ICING
1 tablespoon rose syrup
200 g/1²/₃ cups powdered
   fondant icing sugar
pink food colouring
18 silver dragees, to decorate

*2 baking sheets, greased
and lined
2 piping bags fitted with small
round nozzles/tips and 1 piping
bag fitted with a very small
star nozzle/tip*

makes 18

Preheat the oven to 200°C (400°F) Gas 6.

Spoon the choux pastry dough into one of the piping bags fitted with a round nozzle and pipe 18 rings of 5 cm/2 in diameter and 18 small balls 1 cm/½ in diameter. With clean hands wet your finger and smooth down any peaks from the piping so that the rings and balls are round. Bake in the preheated oven for 10 minutes, then with a sharp knife cut a small slit into each ring and ball and return to the oven for a further 3–5 minutes, until crisp. Cool on a wire rack and then cut each in half.

To make the rose cream, add the rose syrup to the cream and whip to stiff peaks using a whisk. Spoon into the second piping bag fitted with a round nozzle and pipe between the choux ring halves and fill the balls. Reserve some of the cream for decoration.

To make the fondant icing, mix together the rose syrup, powdered fondant icing sugar, 1 tablespoon cold water and a drop of food colouring to achieve a pale pink. Using a round-bladed knife, spread the icing over the tops of the rings. Place a choux ball on top of each ring and ice the top of the balls. Put the reserved rose cream in the piping bag fitted with a very small star nozzle and pipe decorations on the buns, as desired. Top with a silver dragee.

Serve immediately or store in the fridge until needed.

Paris brest – the classic French choux rings – are traditionally made with coffee, but my delicious version features a caramel icing and a rich whiskey cream liqueur filling.

caramel paris brest

1 quantity Choux Pastry
   Dough (see page 27)
caramel curls, to decorate

CREAM LIQUEUR FILLING
300 ml/1¼ cups double/
   heavy cream
1 tablespoon Bailey's or other
   whiskey cream liqueur

CARAMEL FONDANT ICING
200 g/1²/₃ cups powdered
   fondant icing sugar
2 tablespoons caramel sauce

2 baking sheets, greased
and lined
2 piping bags, both fitted with
round nozzles/tips

makes 18

Preheat the oven to 200°C (400°F) Gas 6.

Spoon the choux pastry dough into one of the piping bags and pipe eighteen 6 cm/2½ in diameter rings a small distance apart. With clean hands wet your finger and smooth down any peaks from the piping so that the rings are round. Bake in the preheated oven for 10 minutes, then with a sharp knife cut a small slit into each ring and return to the oven for 3–5 minutes until crisp. Cool on a wire rack and then slice each in half horizontally.

To make the cream filling, add the liqueur to the cream and whip to stiff peaks using a whisk. Spoon into the second piping bag and pipe balls of cream between the choux ring halves.

To make the caramel fondant icing, mix 2 tablespoons cold water with the fondant icing sugar and the caramel sauce until you have a smooth thick icing. Using a round-bladed knife, spread the icing over the tops of the rings and decorate with caramel curls.

Serve immediately or store in the fridge until needed.

These are classic Italian profiteroles, just a little bit tinier. Minute dots of choux pastry, filled with whipped cream and drizzled with a rich chocolate sauce, are piled high in a dessertspoon in individual portions.

chocolate profiteroles

1 quantity Choux Pastry
    Dough (see page 27)
300 ml/1¼ cups double/
    heavy cream

CHOCOLATE SAUCE
80 g/2½ oz. dark chocolate
    (70% cocoa solids)
30 g/2 tablespoons butter
2 tablespoons double/heavy
    cream
2 tablespoons light corn syrup

*2 baking sheets, greased
and lined*
*2 piping bags, both fitted with
round nozzles/tips*

serves 8

Preheat the oven to 200°C (400°F) Gas 6.

Spoon the choux pastry dough into one of the piping bags and pipe eighty small 1 cm/½ in balls onto the prepared baking sheets, a small distance apart. With clean hands wet your finger and smooth down any peaks from the piping so that the balls are round. Bake in the preheated oven for 10 minutes, then with a sharp knife cut a small slit into each ball and return to the oven for 3–5 minutes, until crisp. Let cool on a wire rack and then carefully cut each one in half.

Whip the cream to stiff peaks, spoon it into the second piping bag and fill each profiterole with it.

To make the chocolate sauce, heat the chocolate, butter, cream and syrup in a saucepan until the chocolate has melted and the sauce is smooth and glossy.

To serve, arrange small piles of filled profiteroles in dessertspoons and drizzle with the warm chocolate sauce. Serve immediately.

Millefeuilles – or thousand leaves – is a delicious French pastry that is also known as the Napoleon. In a twist on the traditional filling of vanilla custard, these pastries contain blackcurrant preserve – a sharp fruity burst, perfectly offsetting the cream and sugar dusting.

blackcurrant millefeuilles

MILLEFEUILLES
375-g/13-oz. package all-butter puff pastry (defrosted if frozen)
1 egg beaten
caster/superfine sugar, for sprinkling

FILLING
2 generous tablespoons blackcurrant preserve
200 ml/¾ cup double/heavy cream
icing/confectioners' sugar, for dusting

a baking sheet, greased and lined
a piping bag fitted with a star nozzle/tip

makes 24

Preheat the oven to 180°C (350°F) Gas 4.

On a flour dusted surface, roll out the pastry to a thickness of 3 mm/⅛ in. Cut into six strips of 30 x 4 cm/12 x 2 in and transfer to the baking sheet using a large spatula, leaving a gap between each strip of pastry. Brush with the beaten egg and sprinkle over a little caster/superfine sugar.

Bake in the preheated oven for 12–15 minutes, until the pastry has risen and is golden brown on top. Transfer to a wire rack and let cool completely.

When you are ready to serve, cut each pastry strip into 8 small pieces. Whip the cream to stiff peaks and then spoon into the piping bag. Pipe a row of small cream stars onto half of the pastry squares, top with a small spoonful of blackcurrant preserve then cover with a second pastry square. Repeat until all the pastry squares are filled. Dust the tops with icing/confectioners' sugar.

Serve immediately or store in the fridge until needed.

- 50 g/½ cup blanched hazelnuts
- 30 g/2 tablespoons butter, softened
- 30 g/¼ cup icing/confectioners' sugar
- 25 g/3 tablespoons self-raising/rising flour, plus extra for dusting
- 1 tablespoon beaten egg
- ½ teaspoon vanilla extract
- 25 g/1 oz. white chocolate
- 375-g/13-oz. package all-butter puff pastry (defrosted if frozen)
- 1–2 small ripe pears
- caster/superfine sugar, for dusting

GLAZE
- 1 tablespoon apricot preserve
- juice of ½ a lemon

2 baking sheets, greased and lined
a round fluted cutter (5 cm/2 in diameter)

makes 30

Baked on golden buttery puff pastry, these little pear and hazelnut praline galettes simply melt in the mouth and make the perfect morsel to serve with a cup of tea or coffee.

glazed pear galettes with hazelnut praline

Preheat the oven to 190°C (375°F) Gas 5.

Put the hazelnuts in a food processor and blitz until finely chopped. Add the butter, icing/confectioners' sugar, flour, egg and vanilla extract. Grate in the white chocolate and blitz to form a thick praline paste.

Dust a clean work surface with flour and roll out the pastry to a thickness of 3 mm/⅛ in. Stamp out circles with the cutter and transfer to the baking sheet using a spatula. Use a sharp knife to score an inner circle on each pastry round, about 1 cm/½ in from the edge, taking care not to cut all the way through. Put a spoonful of the praline in the middle of each pastry circle.

Peel, core and finely chop the pears into very thin small slices and place three slices on top of each galette. Sprinkle with a little caster/superfine sugar and bake in the preheated oven for about 12–15 minutes, until the pastry is golden brown and the pears are cooked.

To make the glaze, heat the lemon juice in a saucepan with the apricot preserve. Use a pastry brush to brush the apricot mixture over each tart to glaze. Serve warm or cold.

These pastries will keep in an airtight container for 2 days.

tartlets

PASTRY

110 g/¾ cup plain/all-purpose flour, plus extra for dusting
60 g/½ stick butter
30 g/2 tablespoons caster/superfine sugar
1 egg yolk
a few drops of vanilla extract

CREME PATISSIERE

1 tablespoon cornflour/cornstarch
60 g/⅓ cup caster/granulated sugar
1 egg and 1 egg yolk
100 ml/scant ½ cup milk
150 ml/⅔ cup double/heavy cream
1 vanilla bean, split lengthwise

To ASSEMBLE

200 g/1½ cups summer berries
3 tablespoons apricot preserve
juice of 2 small lemons

a round fluted cutter (6 cm/2½ in diameter)
24 mini tartlet tins/pans, greased
baking parchment
baking beans
a piping bag fitted with a round nozzle/tip

makes 24

These crisp pastry tartlets, filled with classic crème pâtissière and topped with glazed summer berries, are always popular and disappear very quickly whenever I serve them.

summer berry tartlets with vanilla bean cream

To make the pastry, sift the flour into a mixing bowl and rub in the butter until the mixture resembles fine breadcrumbs. Add the sugar, egg yolk and vanilla extract and mix together to a soft dough with your fingers, adding a little cold water if the mixture is too dry. Wrap in clingfilm/plastic wrap and chill in the fridge for 1 hour.

Preheat the oven to 180°C (350°F) Gas 4. On a flour dusted surface, roll out the pastry to a thickness of 3 mm/⅛ in. Stamp out 24 rounds using the cutter and press one into each hole in the pan, trimming away any excess pastry. Chill in the fridge for 30 minutes. Line each pastry case with baking parchment and fill with baking beans. Bake in the preheated oven for 12–15 minutes, until golden brown and crisp. Leave to cool in the pans for 10 minutes, then transfer to a wire rack to cool completely.

To prepare the crème pâtissière, whisk together the cornflour/cornstarch, sugar, egg and egg yolk until creamy. Put the milk, cream and split vanilla bean in a saucepan and bring to the boil. Pour over the egg mixture, whisking all the time. Return to the pan and cook for a few minutes until thick, then remove the vanilla bean. Pass the mixture through a sieve/strainer to remove any lumps and set aside to cool.

To assemble, spoon the crème pâtissière into the piping bag and pipe it into the pastry cases. Top each one with berries. Put the apricot preserve and lemon juice in a small saucepan and heat until blended. Pass through a sieve/strainer to remove any bits and, using a pastry brush, brush the mixture over each tartlet to glaze.

These tartlets are best eaten on the day they are made.

PASTRY

110 g/¾ cup plus 2
    tablespoons plain/
    all-purpose flour, plus
    extra for dusting
60 g/½ stick butter
30 g/2½ tablespoons
    caster/granulated sugar
1 egg yolk

FILLING

3 tablespoons lemon curd or
    other fruit preserve
3 tablespoons mascarpone
50 g/⅓ cup whole blanched
    almonds
50 g/1½ oz. sliced brioche
    or challah bread
60 g/½ stick butter, softened
2 tablespoons caster/
    superfine sugar
1 large egg
1 teaspoon vanilla extract
finely grated zest of 1 lemon

To DECORATE

24 whole blanched almond
    halves (ideally Marcona)
icing/confectioner's sugar,
    for dusting

*a 24-hole/cup mini muffin
tin/pan, greased
a flower-shaped cutter
(6 cm/2½ in diameter)
a piping bag fitted with large
round nozzle/tip*

makes 24

These traditional English tartlets filled with almond paste and fruit preserve, have their origins in Tudor times and are said to have been a favourite of Anne Boleyn's. Similar to bakewell tarts, they make an elegant gift for any hostess.

little maids of honour

To make the pastry, sift the flour into a mixing bowl and rub in the butter until the mixture resembles fine breadcrumbs. Add the sugar and egg yolk and mix together to a soft dough with your fingertips, adding a little cold water if the mixture is too dry. Wrap in clingfilm/plastic wrap and chill in the fridge for 1 hour.

Preheat the oven 180°C (350°F) Gas 4. On a flour dusted surface, roll out the pastry to a thickness of 3 mm/⅛ in. Stamp out 24 flower shapes with the cutter and put one in each hole of the muffin pan, pressing them tightly against the base and side of the pan. Chill in the fridge until needed.

Put ⅓ teaspoon each of lemon curd and mascarpone in the bottom of each pastry case. Put the almonds and brioche in a blender and blitz to a fine crumb. Cream together the butter and sugar, then add the egg, vanilla extract, lemon zest and almond mixture. Mix everything well and then spoon into the piping bag. Pipe a small amount of filling into each tartlet case to fill. Top each one with an almond half and bake in the preheated oven for 12–15 minutes, until golden brown. Dust with icing/confectioners' sugar and serve warm or cold.

These tartlets will keep in an airtight container for 3 days.

The combination of *en vogue* salted caramel and rich chocolate ganache, makes these a sophisticated treat that's guaranteed to delight chocoholics everywhere.

chocolate & salted caramel tartlets

CHOCOLATE PASTRY
80 g/⅔ cup plain/all-purpose
    flour, plus extra for dusting
2 tablespoons cocoa
60 g/½ stick butter
2 tablespoons caster/
    granulated sugar
1 egg yolk

SALTED CARAMEL
100 g/½ cup caster/
    granulated sugar
60 g/½ stick butter
½ teaspoon salt
1 tablespoon double/heavy
    cream

CHOCOLATE GANACHE
100 g/3½ oz. dark chocolate
60 ml/¼ cup double/heavy
    cream
30 g/2 tablespoons butter
1 tablespoon light corn syrup
12 silver dragees, to decorate

*12 mini tartlet tins (6 cm/2½ in
square), greased*

makes 12

To make the pastry, sift the flour and cocoa into a mixing bowl and rub in the butter until the mixture resembles fine breadcrumbs. Add the sugar and egg yolk and mix together to a soft dough with your fingers, adding a little cold water if the mixture is too dry. Wrap in clingfilm/plastic wrap and chill in the fridge for 1 hour.

Preheat the oven to 180°C (350°F) Gas 4. On a flour dusted surface, roll out the pastry to a thickness of 3 mm/⅛ in. Use a sharp knife to cut out 12 squares slightly larger than the baking pans and press one into each pan, trimming away any excess pastry. Chill in the fridge for 30 minutes. Line each tartlet case with baking parchment and fill with baking beans. Bake in the preheated oven for 12–15 minutes, until crisp. Transfer to a wire rack and leave to cool completely.

To make the salted caramel, heat the sugar with 2 tablespoons water in a saucepan set over gentle heat. Remove the pan from the heat as soon the mixture starts to turn golden brown. Add the butter, salt and cream and return to the heat, until the butter has melted. Pour a little of the mixture into the base of each cooled tartlet case.

To make the ganache, put the chocolate, cream and butter in a heatproof bowl set over a pan of simmering water. Take care that the base of the bowl does not touch the water. Stir until the chocolate and butter have melted and blended. Remove from the heat and beat in the syrup. Pour a little into each tartlet case. Leave to partially set then top with a dragee. Leave to set completely before serving.

These tartlets will keep in an airtight container for 3 days.

Caramelized tartes tatin, with their rich buttery pastry and dark sugary caramel, are quite simply delicious. Whilst normally served as a large tart, these individual ones make the perfect sweet treat. You can substitute other fruits, such as apple, pear or pineapple if you prefer.

individual plum tartes tatin

100 g/½ cup caster/
   granulated sugar
50 g/3½ tablespoons butter
6 ripe plums
60 g/2 oz. golden marzipan
plain/all-purpose flour,
   for dusting
375-g/13-oz. package all-butter
   puff pastry, defrosted
   if frozen
custard sauce or whipped
   cream, to serve

a 12-hole/cup bun tin/pan,
greased
a round cutter (9 cm/3½ in
diameter)

makes 12

Preheat the oven to 180°C (350°F) Gas 4.

Put the sugar and butter in a small saucepan and warm over gentle heat, until the sugar dissolves and then allow it to caramelize and turn golden brown, taking care that it does not burn. Remove from the heat immediately and put a spoonful of caramel into each hole of the pan.

Cut the plums in half, remove the stones/pits and place one plum half cut-side up in each hole of the pan. Break the marzipan into 12 pieces of equal size and roll them into balls. Put one ball into each plum, where the stone/pit once was.

On a flour dusted surface, roll the pastry out to a thickness of 3 mm/⅛ in. Stamp out 12 rounds with the cutter. Cover each plum with a pastry round, pressing the pastry tightly into the holes.

Bake in the preheated oven for 12–15 minutes, until the pastry is crisp and the plums are soft. Remove from the oven, let cool for a few minutes then remove each tatin with a spoon and invert.

Serve warm or cold with cream or custard. These tatins are best eaten on the day they are made.

These melt-in-the-mouth tartlets are mini versions of a classic French lemon tart – a delicious combination of light buttery pastry, tangy lemon cream filling and a caramelized sugar topping.

caramelized tartes au citron

TART CASES
110 g/¾ cup plain/all-purpose flour, plus extra for dusting
60 g/½ stick butter
finely grated zest of 2 lemons
2 tablespoons caster/superfine sugar
1 egg yolk

LEMON FILLING
100 ml/⅓ cup double/heavy cream
finely grated zest and juice of 1 lemon
50 g/¼ cup caster/granulated sugar
1 egg
icing/confectioners' sugar, for dusting

20 oval mini tartlet tins/pans (8 cm/3¼ in long), greased
baking parchment
baking beans

makes 20

To make the pastry, sift the flour into a mixing bowl and rub in the butter until the mixture resembles fine breadcrumbs. Add the lemon zest, sugar and egg yolk and mix together to a soft dough with your fingertips, adding a little cold water if the mixture is too dry. Wrap in clingfilm/plastic wrap and chill in the fridge for 1 hour.

Preheat the oven to 180°C (350°F) Gas 4. On a flour dusted surface, roll out the pastry to a thickness of 3 mm/⅛ in. Use a sharp knife to cut out 20 oval pieces of pastry and press one into each tartlet pan, trimming the edges with a sharp knife. Put a piece of baking parchment in each pastry case, fill with baking beans and bake in the preheated oven for 10–15 minutes, until the pastry is crisp. Do not turn off the oven.

To make the filling, whisk together the cream, lemon juice and zest, sugar and egg and pour into each pastry case. Bake in the preheated for 10–15 minutes, until the filling has set. Dust liberally with sifted icing/confectioners' sugar. Caramelize the sugar using a chef's blow torch or under a hot grill/broiler. Leave to cool before serving.

These tartlets will keep for 3 days if stored in an airtight container.

110 g/¾ cup plain/all-purpose flour, plus extra for dusting
60 g/½ stick butter
2½ tablespoons soft dark brown sugar
1 egg yolk

FILLING
100 g/1 cup pecan pieces, plus 24 halves to top the pielets
75 g/⅓ cup caster/granulated sugar
75 g/⅓ cup soft dark brown sugar
1 teaspoon ground cinnamon
1 teaspoon vanilla extract
40 g/3 tablespoons butter
3 tablespoons golden syrup or light corn syrup
1 egg and 1 egg yolk, beaten

a round cutter (6 cm/2½ in a 24 hole/cup mini muffin tin/pan, greased

makes 24

I must confess that this is my favourite recipe in the book. With their crisp buttery pastry and pecans coated in cinnamon caramel, the little pies are heaven sent.

pecan pielets

To make the pastry, sift the flour into a mixing bowl and rub in the butter until the mixture resembles fine breadcrumbs. Add the brown sugar and egg yolk and mix together to a soft dough with your fingertips, adding a little cold water if the mixture is too dry. Wrap in clingfilm/plastic wrap and chill in the fridge for 1 hour. Preheat the oven to 180°C (350°F) Gas 4.

To make the filling, blitz the 100 g/1 cup pecan pieces in a food processor until finely chopped. Heat both the sugars, cinnamon, vanilla extract, butter and syrup until the sugar has dissolved and the butter has melted. Let cool for 10 minutes then beat in the egg and egg yolk. Reserve a third of the syrup mixture and set aside.

On a flour dusted surface, roll out the pastry to a thickness of 3 mm/⅛ in. Stamp out 24 pastry rounds using the cutter and press one into each hole of the pan. Fill each mini pie crust with the chopped pecans and pour in the remaining caramel syrup until each crust is full. Top each pie with a pecan half.

Bake in the preheated oven for 12–15 minutes, until the filling is set. Take the pies out of the pan whilst still warm. This is easiest done with a teaspoon, pushing the spoon down the side of each pie in the pan. Put the pies on a wire rack with a sheet of foil underneath to catch any drips. Heat the reserved syrup gently and brush it over the tops of the pies using a pastry brush. Serve warm or cold.

These pielets will keep for 3 days if stored in an airtight container.

desserts

60 g/⅓ cup ground almonds
60 g/⅓ cup unsalted
    pistachio kernels
150 g/1 cup icing/
    confectioners' sugar
90 g/⅓ cup egg whites (about
    3 eggs – retain the yolks)
75 g/⅓ cup caster/superfine
    sugar
green food colouring

ICE CREAM
3 egg yolks
90 g/⅓ cup plus 1 tablespoon
    caster/granulated sugar
100 g/generous ½ cup
    unsalted pistachio kernels
200 ml/¾ double/heavy cream
100 ml/½ cup milk
½ teaspoon vanilla extract
green food colouring

2 baking sheets, lined with
baking parchment
a piping bag fitted with a large
round nozzle/tip
an ice cream maker (optional)

makes 15

Pâtissèries such as Ladurée are to be credited with the delightful resurgence of this chic French treat. Here petite pistachio macarons are filled with homemade ice cream.

pistachio macarons

Put the ground almonds, pistachios and icing/confectioners' sugar in a food processor and blitz to a very fine powder. Sift into a bowl and return any pieces of nut that do not pass through the sieve/strainer to the blender, blitz and sift again. Whisk the egg whites to stiff peaks and then add the caster/superfine sugar a spoonful at a time until the mixture is smooth and glossy. Add the pistachio powder a third at a time with a few drops of food colouring. Fold in with a spatula until the mixture just holds a peak. Spoon the mixture into the piping bag and pipe thirty 5 cm/2 in rounds onto the prepared baking sheets. Set aside for 1 hour so that a skin forms.

Preheat the oven to 170°C (325°F) Gas 3. Bake the macarons in the preheated oven for 15–20 minutes, until firm. Leave to cool on the baking sheets.

To make the ice cream, whisk together the egg yolks and caster/granulated sugar until thick and creamy. Finely chop the pistachios. Heat the milk and cream in a saucepan with the pistachios and bring to the boil. Pour the hot cream mixture over the eggs, add the vanilla extract and a few drops of food colouring, whisking all the time, then return to the pan and cook until thickened. Chill completely. Churn in an ice cream maker until frozen or put in a freezerproof tub in the freezer and whisk every 30 minutes until frozen.

To assemble, sandwich together two macarons with slightly softened ice cream and serve immediately.

These crisp yet sticky mini meringues are bursting with tropical flavours. Hints of rum, coconut and pineapple will transport you to sunnier climes in one little sugary mouthful.

pineapple pavlovas with rum

MERINGUES

2 egg whites

115 g/²/₃ cup caster/superfine sugar

TO ASSEMBLE

2 tablespoons long shredded coconut

2 rings canned or fresh pineapple

2 tablespoons coconut rum, such as Malibu

125 ml/½ cup double/heavy cream

2 baking sheets, lined with baking parchment
a piping bag fitted with a large star nozzle/tip

makes 18

Preheat the oven to 140°C (275°F) Gas 1.

Put the egg whites and sugar in a heatproof bowl set over a pan of simmering water. Whisk for about 3–5 minutes, until the sugar has dissolved. Remove from the heat and whisk to stiff peaks.

Use a spatula to put the meringue into the piping bag and pipe eighteen 5 cm/2 in blobs on the prepared baking sheets and then pipe 5 high stars of meringue around the edge of each, leaving a gap in the middle which will hold the cream filling.

Bake in the preheated oven for about 1–1½ hours, until the meringues are dried and crisp. Leave the meringues to cool completely.

When you are ready to serve, toast the coconut in a dry frying pan/skillet, until it starts to turn golden brown (take care that it does not burn). Finely chop the pineapple and soak it in the coconut rum. Whip the cream to stiff peaks and place a small spoonful in the middle of each meringue. Top with the rum-soaked pineapple and toasted coconut. Serve immediately or store in the fridge until needed.

BASE
180 g/6 oz. butter shortcake
    cookies
70 g/5 tablespoons butter,
    melted

TOPPING
200 ml/¾ cup crème fraîche
    or sour cream
200 g/¾ cup mascarpone
100 g/3½ oz. white chocolate,
    melted and cooled
100 g/¾ cup raspberries

TO ASSEMBLE
20 raspberries
light corn syrup
gold leaf
popping candy (optional)

*a loose-based baking tin/pan
(20 x 15 cm/8 x 6 in),
greased and lined*

makes 20

Rich, creamy cheesecake is always a favourite. Served in tiny squares and topped with a gilded raspberry, it is sure to delight at any party. If you want to give your guests a surprise treat, you can add a fun popping candy topping.

white chocolate & raspberry cheesecakes

To make the base, put the cookies in a food processor and blitz to a fine crumb. Transfer to a bowl, pour in the melted butter and mix together. Spoon the cookie base into the prepared pan and press down firmly with the back of a spoon.

To make the cheesecake topping, whisk together the crème fraîche and mascarpone. Fold in the cooled melted chocolate and raspberries with a spatula and spoon the mixture into the pan. Level the surface of the cheesecake with a spatula and chill in the fridge for 3 hours, until set.

When you are ready to serve, remove the cheesecake from the pan. Cut into 20 squares, using a sharp knife. Place a raspberry in the middle of each square and use a pastry brush to brush with a little corn syrup. Decorate with gold leaf by pressing it into the syrup. Sprinkle with popping candy (if using) and serve immediately or store in the fridge until needed.

CITRUS CURD

80 ml/⅓ cup lemon and lime juice (roughly 2 lemons and 3 limes)
60 g/½ stick butter
115 g/⅓ cup plus 1 tablespoon caster/granulated sugar
2 eggs

CHOCOLATE SHORTCAKE

60 g/½ cup plain/all-purpose flour, plus extra for dusting
1 tablespoon cocoa powder
60 g/½ stick butter, chilled
25 g/2 tablespoons caster/granulated sugar

MERINGUE

100 g/½ cup caster/superfine sugar
40 ml/2½ tablespoons light corn syrup
2 large egg whites

24 fluted tartlet tins/pan (5 cm/2 in diameter), greased
baking parchment
baking beans
a piping bag fitted with a large large star nozzle

makes 24

These little pies are full of tangy citrus curd, topped with a fluffy meringue and encased in crisp chocolate shortcake.

mini lemon & lime meringue pies

To make the citrus curd, put the juice, butter and sugar in a heatproof bowl set over a pan of simmering water and whisk until the sugar has dissolved. Beat the eggs and add to the butter mixture, whisking continuously, until the mixture thickens. Pass through a sieve/strainer to remove any lumps. Let cool and store in the fridge until needed.

To make the pastry, sift the flour and cocoa into a mixing bowl and rub in the butter with your fingertips, until the mixture resembles fine breadcrumbs. Add the sugar, and a little cold water if needed, and work the pastry with your hands until it comes together into a ball. Wrap in cling film/plastic wrap and chill in the fridge for 1 hour.

Preheat the oven to 180°C (350°F) Gas 4. On a flour dusted surface, roll out the pastry to a thickness of about 3 mm/⅛ in. Cut out rounds of pastry slightly larger than the tart pans with a sharp knife. Press a round of pastry into each pan, trimming away any excess with a sharp knife. Transfer to the fridge for 30 minutes, then remove, line each pan with baking parchment and fill with baking beans. Bake in the preheated oven for 10–15 minutes, until the tarts cases are crisp. Turn out onto a wire rack and let cool. Fill each case with the citrus curd.

To make the meringue, heat the sugar, syrup and 2½ tablespoons water in a saucepan, until the sugar has dissolved and bring to the boil. Put the egg whites in a bowl and whisk to a stiff peak. Pour in the hot sugar syrup and whisk continuously until the meringue is cold. Spoon the meringue into the piping bag and pipe a swirl on top of the curd.

Lightly brown the meringue with a chef's blow torch or under a grill/broiler. Serve immediately or store in the fridge until needed.

CAKE BASE

60 g/½ stick butter
60 g/⅓ cup caster/granulated
  sugar
1 egg
45 g/⅓ cup self-raising/
  self-rising flour
15 g/1 tablespoon cocoa

CHOCOLATE SHELLS

300 g/10½ oz. dark chocolate

MOUSSE FILLING

150 g/5½ oz. white chocolate
225 ml/1 scant cup
  double/heavy cream

*a 24-hole/cup mini muffin
tin/pan, lined with paper cases
a piping bag fitted with a large
star nozzle/tip*

makes 24

These little cakes look impressive but the delicate chocolate shells are very easy to prepare. Filled with sponge cake and white chocolate mousse, these are a chocoholics delight.

triple chocolate mousse cakes

Preheat the oven to 180°C (350°F) Gas 4.

Beat together the butter and sugar in a bowl with a whisk. Add the egg and beat again. Sift in the flour and cocoa and fold into the mixture. Put a spoonful in each paper case. Bake in the preheated oven for 10–12 minutes, until the cakes spring back to the touch. Let cool on a wire rack.

Cut twenty-four 10 cm/4 in square pieces of baking parchment. Melt the chocolate in a heatproof bowl set over a pan of barely simmering water (do not let the base of the bowl touch the water). Using a pastry brush, brush a thick layer of chocolate over the middle of each square. Do not brush all the way to the edge and reserve a little for decoration. Peel the paper cases off of the cakes and put a cake in the middle of each chocolate sheet. Put the chocolate sheets in the (cleaned) muffin pan and press down on the cakes so that the sides of the baking parchment sit up around the edge. To make the mousse, melt the white chocolate as above and let cool. Whip the cream and fold it into the cooled chocolate. Spoon the white chocolate mousse into the piping bag and pipe a swirl on top of each cake. Drizzle with the reserved melted dark chocolate. Chill for 3 hours, then peel away the paper to release the chocolate cups. Serve immediately or store in the fridge until needed.

These tiny treats boast all the flavours of everyone's favourite Italian dessert in one mouthful. Filled with fluffy mascarpone cream and espresso coffee, these mini roulades make a sophisticated dessert.

tiramisù roulade

ROULADE SPONGE CAKE

150 ml/²/₃ cup double/heavy cream

2 teaspoons instant coffee, dissolved in 1 tablespoon hot water

70 g/½ cup cocoa

5 eggs, separated

120 g/½ cup plus 1 tablespoon caster/granulated sugar

icing/confectioners' sugar, for dusting

TIRAMISU FILLING

300 ml/1¼ cups double/heavy cream

2 tablespoons icing/confectioners' sugar

2 tablespoons coffee liqueur

170 g/²/₃ cup mascarpone

2 teaspoons instant coffee, dissolved in hot water

2 baking tins/pans
(33 x 23 cm/13 x 9 in),
greased and lined

makes 18

Preheat the oven to 180°C (350°F) Gas 4.

To prepare the sponge cake, put the cream and coffee in a small saucepan and heat gently. Add the cocoa and mix to a smooth paste. Set aside to cool. Whisk the egg yolks and sugar together until doubled in size and very light and creamy. Beat the cocoa paste into the egg yolk mixture. In a separate bowl, whisk the egg whites to stiff peaks, then fold into the cocoa and egg mixture. Divide the mixture between the prepared pans and bake in the preheated oven for 12–15 minutes, until the cakes spring back to the touch. Dust two large sheets of baking parchment (larger than the size of the cakes) with icing/confectioners' sugar and turn the cakes out onto them. Leave to cool completely.

When you are ready to fill the roulade, trim away the crusts from the edges of the sponges and cut each sponge into 9, to give a total of 18 rectangles.

To make the tiramisù filling, whip the cream to stiff peaks, then beat in the icing/confectioners' sugar, coffee liqueur, mascarpone and dissolved coffee. Spread the filling over each sponge rectangle with a round-bladed knife and roll up using a small sheet of baking parchment to assist you (so that the icing/confectioners' sugar dusted layer is on the outside of the roulade). Do not worry if the sponge cake cracks as it will be held together with the filling.

Serve immediately or store in the fridge until needed.

POSSET

600 ml/2½ cups double/
   heavy cream
200 g/1 cup caster/granulated
   sugar
finely grated zest and juice
   of 2 small oranges and
   2 lemons
2 teaspoons finely chopped
   fresh mint

MADELEINES

2 eggs
80 g/⅓ cup caster/granulated
   sugar
100 g/¾ cup plus 1
   tablespoon self-
   raising/rising flour
1 tablespoon honey
zest of 1 orange
1 teaspoon vanilla extract
100 g/7 tablespoons butter,
   melted and cooled

12 small shot glasses
2 x 20-hole/cup mini Madeleine
tins/pans, well greased

serves 12

Posset has its origins in Medieval England and this syllabub-like dessert is still popular today. Served in small glasses with a side order of dainty orange madeleines, this dish is a must for elegant dinner parties.

mini madeleines with a citrus posset

To make the posset, put the cream, sugar, orange and lemon zests and mint in a saucepan and heat for about 3–5 minutes, until the sugar has dissolved. Bring to the boil and then strain into a large jug/pitcher through a fine mesh sieve/strainer to remove the mint and zest. Whisk in the orange and lemon juices then pour into the glasses. Chill in the fridge for 3–4 hours, until the posset is set.

To make the madeleines, whisk together the eggs and sugar until light and creamy. Sift in the flour, add the honey, orange zest and vanilla extract and whisk again. Pour in the cooled melted butter and fold in using a spatula. Spoon the mixture into the piping bag. Chill in the fridge for 1 hour.

Preheat the oven to 180°C (350°F) Gas 4. Pipe a little of the mixture into each hole in the madeleine pan and bake in the preheated oven for 10–15 minutes, until golden brown. (If you only have one madeleine pan bake in batches, storing the uncooked batter in the fridge whilst the first batch is cooking.) Turn the madeleines out onto a wire rack to cool.

Serve a glass of posset with 3 madeleines for each serving (you will have a few extra madeleines leftover for second helpings). The madeleines and posset are both best eaten on the day they are made.

index